THE ROBINSON BROTHERS ADVENTURE

BY DONITA J. CLARK
ILLUSTRATED BY NAVI' ROBINS

Copyright © 2019 by **Donita Clark**

All rights reserved. This book or any portion thereof may not be reproduced or used in any manner whatsoever without the express written permission of the publisher except for the use of brief quotations in a book review or scholarly journal.

C.J., the founder, loves to do outside chores for money. He was always looking for ways to make money.

C.J. and D.J. began by asking their parents to do chores. C.J. and D.J. were excited about getting paid to do the things they loved.

They went house to house looking for things to be done.

C.J. and D.J. saved money to buy more equipment for their business

www.ingramcontent.com/pod-product-compliance
Lightning Source LLC
Chambersburg PA
CBHW040753020526
44118CB00042B/2932